The simplicity of the words define the poet's craft as [Saha] chooses clipped lines, concise fragments to let the light within his stanzas flow. And his images are of everyday life lacquered with the beauty of thoughts... [Saha] practices this cartography not just with words, but heart, too.

The New Indian Express

FUGITIVE WORDS

Amit Shankar Saha

HAWAKAL

HAWAKAL

Published by Hawakal Publishers
185 Kali Temple Road, Nimta, Kolkata 700049
India

Email info@hawakal.com
Website www.hawakal.com

First edition June, 2019

Copyright © Amit Shankar Saha 2019

Cover concept: Steve Menezes
Cover art: Anindita Bose

All rights reserved. No part of this publication may be reproduced or transmitted (other than for purposes of review/critique) in any form or by any means, electronic or mechanical, including photocopy, recording, or any information storage and retrieval system without prior permission in writing from the publisher or the copyright holder where applicable. The author asserts his moral right to be identified as the author of his work.

ISBN: 978-93-87883-69-7

Price: 300 INR | USD 8.99

For
Ahaan

Memory and Grief

Amit S. Saha explores memory and desire through the lens of loss and despair. The grief is beyond personal. Some of these poems are political but only in the sense that one mourns when one's country is in disrepair. Saha tactfully employs images that indicate the physical presence of grief, such as the lump in the throat one gets at the sudden loss of a loved one. He even "attempts" a feminist poem, but his mother has passed as depicted in it, and therefore he is unable. The image of the deceased mother is a cultural manifestation. The poem is archetypal commentary on the death of humankind's most warm, emotional side. This blockage of memory is more than what it seems to illicit. Grief represents the passage of time and its storage within the neural structures of our brains. Mind and body are not dualistic, as Descartes suggested, but part and parcel of one another. What the body experiences, the mind records. We can remember the Mother, but our humanity depends on actual conversation with her. Saha addresses the memory in a compassionate yet frightening way. His approach is human as it reaches into those dark fugitive lands of our being.

This is where the words hide. Where do we find them? Saha is an expert in economy of words, picking them and sorting them in the most emotive and empowering way. They speak for more than Saha himself. These "fugitive words" are literal fugitives, escaping criminal proceedings brought against them, yet they are metaphorical fugitives, as in escapees who must be rounded up in the poem itself. Personas speak through the poems themselves in a candid, yet not directly, confessional way. How clever it is to humanize one's poetry.

The beautiful use of seasonal imagery and natural events make these poems timeless. They are merciful yet imbued with the darkness that springs from that mercy. The world as we experience it is a disease. In the language of Christianity, we are "fallen." Saha tells us of the rain. In poems such as "Forgetting the Rains," we see a human-all-too-human Nature as she pervades the privacy of moments, instilling them with depth beyond our casual experience. Saha's poems are sad and pleasant as they lust for the sheer personal being of Nature herself—only in the sense that Nature would allow it.

As we travel these poems, we are introduced to a scientific understanding that is compatible with humanist spirituality. Spirituality, properly understood, is the drive to develop meaning in the world and sublimate it. By nature, poetry is spiritual. However, Saha is not explicitly spiritual. His depth in quest for meaning reveals itself in his images as they scatter on the page in a buoyant yet dark playfulness. He admits that a poem cannot be great. He is aware that poetry is language, not reality. Like memory, poetry is a presence on the page of being.

These poems are delightful and thoughtful. As the reader peruses them, their deepest longings are fugitive within the heart. What escapes between the lines is a sense of gloom, but not of hopelessness. The poet does not judge life. He cannot. To do so would indeed require greatness only God can harvest. Saha is no god and he is not trying to create a world from nothing. He is employing the depth of being to speak for the truth as it resurrects on the page. While the poems are not spiritual in essence, they convey a lust for meaning and the search itself through grief, memory, longing, and wanting to remember. Saha is a friend of paradox as well. One might say he travels with quantum superposition if a man can reach quantum states. A man cannot reach quantum states, but his fugitive words will—if he thrusts his mind into the dark squandering of our existence.

Dustin Pickering
Houston, Texas
June 10, 2019

Acknowledgements

I thankfully acknowledge the editors of the following venues for being the first publisher of a few of my poems: *The Pangolin Review*, *The Winnow Magazine*, *Shot Glass Journal*, *The Narrow Road*, *The Kolkata Review*, *The New Indian Express*, *Get Bengal*, *Coldnoon Travel Poetics*, *The Wagon Magazine*, *Woman Inc.*, *Yawp*, *Setu Bilingual Journal*, *Poetry: At the Heart of the Nation*, *Hakara Journal*, *Best Indian Poetry* 2018, *Indifaring Muse*, *Love & Politics,* and *Equiverse Space*. Some of these poems were written on prompts of NAPOWRIMO/ GLOPOWRIMO given by Facebook poetry groups like The Significant League, Celebrating World Poetry Writing Month with WE and Global Poetry Writing Month with the Missing Slate.

I owe a wealth of gratitude to my fellow poet Ananya Chatterjee for inspiring many of the poems contained in this volume. I am also grateful to the co-founders of *Rhythm Divine Poets*: Sufia Khatoon and Anindita Bose, for their constant support. I thank Dustin Pickering for writing the foreword. Thanks to Ra Sh for the blurb. I am thankful to Philip Nikolayev, Nikita Parik, Jagari Mukherjee, Kushal Poddar, Mallika Bhaumik, Lopa Banerjee, Sanjukta Dasgupta, Sharmila Ray, Nabina Das, Saima Afreen, Duane Vorhees, Aakriti Kuntal, Ruth Pal Chaudhuri, Ampat Koshy, Satbir Chadha, Santosh Bakaya, Rituparna Khan, Uday Saha, Partha Chatterjee, Smeetha Bhoumik, Sujatha Mathai and Asoke Kumar Mitra for their keen insights and interest in my work. I thank M Padma Shri whose painting inspired the poem, "A Warli Artwork." I am especially thankful to my teacher, Steve Menezes, who conceptualized the cover design, and Anindita Bose, who painted the cover art.

Special thanks go to my mother, father, uncle, my brother Jyoti and his wife, Indu, for believing in me. Also thanks go to my university and its Vice-Chancellor, Prof. Manjusha Tarafdar, for the support and encouragement. And last, but not the least, I thank *Hawakal Publishers* for having faith in my work.

CONTENTS

My Words	15
The Waterfall	16
A Warli Artwork	17
Thorns	18
Winter in Bolpur	19
Snow Flake	20
Convalescent	21
The Three Quarter Moon	22
Spices	23
Paisley	25
Your Grandmother's Sari	26
This Bijoya	28
Autumning	29
Grey Love	30
Rai	31
Brinda	32
Binodini	33
The Outsider	34
Trafficked	35
Late Mother's Day Celebration	37
Lahore Bomb Blast Series	39
The Hind Shawl Repairing House	44
A Poem for Dark Times	45

At Dusk	46
The Eyes	47
Language Lab	48
Scattering	49
Abyss	50
Disguise	51
Decadence	52
Atoms of My Psyche	53
Caterpillar Train	54
Room Cat	55
Bubble Universe	56
Blindness	57
Blind Man's Rainbow	58
Forgetting the Rains	60
Lake Bled	61
Written at a Tea Stall on Sriniketan Road	62
Rain Within	64
Fugitive Words	65
The Air That Ate Eternity	67
Ajar	68
On that Moment of Horripilation when Our Cold Feet Touch	69
Like a Tree	70
Transformation	71
Olfaction	72
Fronds	73
Shell	74
The Greatest Love Poem	75
The City in the Night Time	76
The Last Obsession	77
Measuring Emptiness	78

The Water Diviner	79
Building the Pacific Ocean	80
Spectrum	81
Windows	82
Sleeping	83
Saving the Bridge	84
The Lost Pigeons of Summer	85
Elephant	86
Into the Darkness	87
Long Night	88
Small Hours	89
The Tumour in My Head	90
About a Homicide	91
Lost Object	93
Ruminations from a Sick Bed	94
Fermentation	96
Extinction	97

My Words

Trees squat on tall grasses,
a pond cries for drowned souls,
plantains droop into muddy sleep,
fishes breathe hyacinth dreams,
weeds and stones outlive the night,

the lily will shy to flower here:

my words, those that live in huts by the tracks,
who owns their lives in this light of dusk?

They clamber into my poems
like a broken bridge half-way into a river,
like a broken roof half-way into a house.

The Waterfall

At the waterfall the wind ruffles
the hair of water, shaking off drops
like flakes of dandruff from the head
of a crevice top. How unkempt?
It befits the rugged terrain though,
where sprays of Dionysiac thoughts
get frozen in the cold lake
by the hill like thawing frost.
And under a violet sky
with the air of smoke-like clouds
there flutters with a greenish tinge
the purple faith of a violent heart.

A Warli Artwork

A Warli artwork you did long ago
where you depict an evening scene,
where skeleton men and women
dance and skip around a peacock,
a white crescent moon on a dark
background creates a luminescence.

There's so much serenity captured
within the wooden frame that I
wonder if these centipedes of
acrylic strokes on cloth actually
depict a real scene from a real place.

Perhaps it is all imagination:
just as we imagine there is calm
before the storm when actually
it is the last gasp that art takes
before its subject is destroyed.

Thorns

The meteorologists announce
there's depression in my latitudes.

Darkness climbs over cloaked canopy
as rainclouds gather like prickly heat.

Lights gawk through funnels of basking flies
and wink with flaccid leaves.

A wind carries whispers
of desolation amidst the trees.

The mind chews on malignant risks
of treading on doldrums of memories.

A depression is not a depression
unless it kills, so I die

everyday. We hold the ends of winter
quilt to fold it one last time.

Winter in Bolpur

It never snows in Bolpur.
The midnight of my hair
starts to fade.
On foggy streets
a winter dawns
with shelterless death.
Winter freezes
something in my gut.
I switch on the lights
to search for feelings.
All missing replies
huddle in my dark room.
I sleep like a child
and let monsters lie
under the bed.
I shave the heads
of mourning words.
In the snows of Bolpur
a midnight express
chugs to Gaya.

Snow Flake

Today it is raining in Bolpur.
I put out the light,
open the window
and listen to the sound
of raindrops.
One little drop
climbs through the grills
of the window,
enters the room
and sits in the dark.
In the morning
it lies supine,
spread on the floor.
I step on it,
killing it instantly.
I sprint out
into the day
and a never before seen
flake of snow
travels in the summer heat.

Convalescent

A little ahead of Shyambati,
night sheds lights to reveal

its mysterious shape.
It's like walking into

somebody's confession.
At the bend of Ratan Palli

dogs smell darkness and run
after *totos*. Headlights of

motorcycles impale the road.
A leader's elegies become

owls hooting into wee hours.
Periyar's water table drowns

wolves of my bedimmed grief.
This banyan growing in my

mouth will not melt tonight.
This ichor is a malady.

The Three-Quarter Moon

The three-quarter moon in my mobile
at thirty-three degree Celsius
is a caricature of the real.

The three-quarter moon is a *jahaji*
who crossed the black waters of the Atlantic
to work in the sugar plantations.

The three-quarter moon is a beachcomber
who imitated the songs of the birds
in cross-continental migrations.

The three-quarter moon is a sabre-toothed creature
of a world where god was not yet born
and there was no imagination.

The three-quarter moon is where we existed
when the three-quarter moon did not exist
and the whole creation was just fiction.

Spices

In Paradise Pickle Factories
smell of grandmothers sits
cross-legged to tell stories
of spices who went on long
voyages across the seas.

In that long lost past
forefathers and foremothers
of fenugreek and cardamom
traded in gold and silver
in the bazaars of Persia.

And one day that long ago
a handful of restless mustard
seeds migrated into the west
and mixed with the gypsy
lands swarthy and pungent.

Today in my turmeric mind
when I recall their memory,

listening to smells, smelling stories,
tastes of a bay-leaf past
seep in with all the oils and cloves.

Paisley

You, who will find her one evening smiling
at me while wishing an untimely goodbye
and leave me with you under a roof roofless,
know that her footsteps echo an ancient
amnesia of the beginning where
she left paisleys of footprints on the leaves
for generations of my rebirth to see
and not recognize the fossils of the past
gleaming in the perpetual monsoon rains
on alluvial plains of my geography,
where paisley shaped rivers meander like lost
inhabitants of a civilization
that the archaeologists forgot to dig
and record in the annals of history.

Your Grandmother's Sari

You wore your grandmother's sari today.
Fuchsia and silver coloured sari,
a family heirloom passed on to you.
I have heard that your grandmother played cards
with your college friends – most interesting.
My grandmother too has left some saris;
my mother wears them now. My grandmother
used to have betel leaf with lime at one
point in time but she gave up that habit
later in life. There's an old betel nut
cracker somewhere in my house. All these mark
the passing away of a generation
and what they have left behind, that which we
inherit as curlicues of the past.
What if our grandmothers come back one day
from a parallel universe to re-
claim all that they have left behind and find
how wars have eaten up the family
heirlooms or partition devoured them, how...
but these are negative thoughts and I must

not harbour them. So, I apologize
to fuchsia and silver memories
of grandmothers, betel nuts, saris and
parallel universes for the same.

This Bijoya

A late hour interacts
with your *kamala* sari.
I walk into
a cafe of thought,
order a wok
of Banalata Sen.
Ashwin's Durga bids
goodbye on *Bijoya*
like a waiter who
leaves me with a bill.

Autumning

Whenever I come back
to the love-struck city
I remember you.
In this month of *Ashwin*
Durga too comes back,
autumn comes back,
a memory comes back.
But it crumples and shrinks
into a dark corner
as my house fills
with a migrant sadness.
It won't come out,
it fears persecution.
When my sad soul
kneels before you,
don't call it a refugee
and shoot it in the head.

Grey Love

In this aged *Hemanta*
when a grin-faced poet
enquires in a grim voice
about my denuded self,

I undo my smoke-leaden
tresses onto my yellow skin
to hide the marks of *Basanta*
left by a migrating spring.

Won't the poet love me now,
whisper those old sweet nothings,
paint poems in green and red,
make pregnant the broken nest?

If grey love is blasphemy
then the seasons too are sins.

Rai

A fading sleep clusters
with the kohl in my eyes.
Drops of dream leave the lids,
escape the nape and fly.
Dying buds mourn precocious love.
Colours of *Basant Utsav*
make up for the absence
of the blush at your touch.
I, your Rai, why wake up
to uncoil my being from us?

Brinda

In the forest of Brindavan
colours of estrangement I seek.
Colour of a fallen hibiscus
colours my misleading feet.
Colour of a lonely night
becomes the colour of my eyes.
How many blinks will bring the day?
How many blinks will cause sunrise?
Colours of the forest green
grin from leaves while the clouds weep.
Colours sail within my veins
wind-blown by a stormy breath.
Colours fade into the pale
like a memory after death.

Binodini

A sprinkle of dusk smears my face
My heart is a room where I light the moon

The *saba* of a flute steps into my breath
Colours of his voice pour in the night

My Jugal is a muezzin who calls the *azaan*
I kneel for *namaz* in the noise of his hue

A fleet of feet sails from the *ghats* of Mathura
Love is a flight to a mosque in Medina

The Outsider

On World Valentine's Day
I decide to write a feminist poem.
I imagine myself as a woman,
oppressed and depressed,
who has escaped the oven,
who stirs her imagination within utensils,
pastes it on tins of provisions,
colours it with her menstrual blood,
hides it behind nights of unconsent.
I imagine my imagination
stunted by language of power,
and all the words I birth
become husbands and fathers.
I imagine my imagination
struggling within bellies and breasts.
I imagine my imagination
suffocating behind eyelids of unrest,
until it congeals into a tumour in my head.
I cannot write a feminist poem
for my mother is dead.

Trafficked

I undress
as I write this.
There goes the last
thread from my body.
In the corners
of every room
I shed a sigh
of missing girls,
who are supposed
to be long dead.
Between the furrows
of the fields
my eyes roam.
Greens become grey
far away.
Fertility consorts
with the rich loam.
When it's pitch dark
you can see us
amidst the ploughshares.

Patrols screech
at my naked borders,
search all my moans.

Late Mother's Day Celebration

Your mother reads a poem you wrote,
she wears black of some mourning.

While passing Benaras Bridge near Sorting
                              Yard Cabin
I see a house of three mothers with all the
                         children missing.

Beside a village pond some mothers
sit to watch the tail end of a dull day crawl into
                                    an evening,

others wash in the waters the siesta of their skin.

On the far end of my hind sight
is the pink house of my cousin,
whose mother never returned
from the School of Tropical Medicine.

Mothers are like nations:
they make us emotional.

If you trace an outline map of her
you will find in her geography
rivers of her mystical history.

Lahore Bomb Blast Series

I
And I have memories
of those few months,
which no bomb blast
can blow to smithereens.
I ask the day's victims
as they pass by,
listen, answer,
where do memories go
when pierced by splinters?
They look at me
but don't reply
for their eyes are blasted
and their mouths hold no speech.
And in my mind
the remnant of
silence remains.

II
When I close my eyes
my mind flies
like the scattered brain
of a blast victim.
The blasted memories
scoot and stick
at various places
of the bombed site
as forensic evidence
of your presence
in my mind.
They don't let me open my eyes
for if I do so
they will know
that I did not die
and the post-mortem
will be delayed.

III
You know how it is to die
blasted by a bomb.
You don't have time to sigh
when you live that moment.
And the bird
that fornicated
with the bird
in my mind
leaves a trail of blood.
You know how the wars have
split our selves in two
and when they release
the list of victims
they name me as you.

IV
That moment when in love
I gave you my all,
even the last drop
percolated in you.
You arched your back
and a civilization grew
underneath its dome.
Why did you moan?
Did I smother your breasts?
How many people mourned
when our unborn children
got bombed in Lahore?

V
At the end of the night
it is the lone light bulb
that stays burning
while all the other lights
have died gradually.
This lone light bulb
we send to face
the blast of the sun
that drowns the little glow
of this lone bulb.
You say, switch it off.
I switch it off.
But something still burns
and the glow remains
at the site of the bomb
blasted in our hearts.

The Hind Shawl Repairing House

Refu *chacha* became all frantic
when he heard the leader say
that the newly elected government
will impose the dreaded NRC.
He said that he would be forced to
leave without any place to go.

I have a *kameez* in my closet,
a dull garment I no longer wear,
which once got ripped long back,
and he mended it so well
that no naked eye could make out
the invisible tear in the fabric.

A Poem for Dark Times

Let us presume there exists
a poem that I want to write.
Let us search for that poem tonight.

Let us plagiarize a chunk of verse
from a Hindu poem and profane it
with the lines of a Muslim poem.

Let us put out the light and sing
the words of that poem and see
if the words kill each other and cease to be.

At Dusk

Two girls play hide-and-seek
in a rail track house.
Brambles grow on abandoned hours,
a stream sways boats to long-term sleep,
clothes smile from voyeur stiles,
a crooked tree mothers an orphan doll,
an old woman on a broken roof
stares and stares at passing time,
a crowd of lights shouts in the eyes,
a chiaroscuro dies on the wall.
This mofussil life will wither and fade
and no difference to you it will make.
What if I climb a railway bridge
and jump from there to cause a blip?
The world will sink into your mind,
it will be dark and we will sing.

The Eyes

A slow train at Talit
looks befuddled at fields
of ripe-green memories.

Under a lame grey cloud
a late evening descends
into hurried darkness.

But the asthmatic night
of urgent forgetting
strains to take every breath.

Your eyes unsight while I
search for the person who
hides and writes my poems.

Language Lab

In the afternoon the rear window
of the language lab lets in the sun,
which shimmies through the silken threads
of the old spider's cobweb.
Shapes of window frames on the floor
at the darkening bright end
make for an interesting view
of self-introspection by the room.
When I shut the door and the fans
slowly stop their whirling motion,
something settles in the room to
spend the night in desolation.

Scattering

A few grey spots consume the day,
sultry thoughts swap sundry others,
a forgotten *mohona* moans
in the cavity of my chest.
The night of your heart sparks the sky,
a cool breeze moves the dull lamp shade,
an unborn storm breathes in the wind,
drops of sweat slither on my nape.
If I remember you tonight,
it is because my fugitive
memory escapes the flaccid hours
spent on the banks of forgetfulness.

Abyss

A lone light travels swiftly
down the bend of a long highway
chased by the darkness of night
into an abyss of unsight.

See how a fast-approaching train
imitates a fast-approaching
memory of you – the friction
of its wheels grating in the mind.

Missing you is like winter
spent hidden under an old quilt
in the dark, without a torch,
without being spied, without being sought.

Disguise

When I leave the city,
the horn of the engine
at Rishra station reminds me
of how I have become
a mercenary poet who
writes poems on leave-taking
while the train passes by
The Phosphate Company.
So many dwellings pass by,
places where we don't dwell,
rooms where we don't sleep,
ponds where we don't bathe,
terraces where we don't
go to talk hidden in attics.
We constantly dwell in disguise
like strangers to the eyes.

Decadence

A betrayal of clouds looms
over the parcel office
at Bolpur station. A red
shirt boy kicks a ball in
a circumference of his
imagination. Noise of
birds intersperse with sounds of
announcements. A voyeur
light hides and spies and slowly
murders ants that grow wings.
Tonight, I will call you
from the embryo of guilt.
In the darkness, decadence
leaves your body naked.
There is no betrayal if
we both betray each other.

Atoms of My Psyche

Butterflies in the grass swing from stems,
two storks flap over electric poles,
the moor by the marshland moans dissent,
far on the circumference traffic plies,
a warm wind makes my eyelids blink,
a breeze makes a long leaf discontent.
From outside the transparent panes
spying trees look into my face,
shaking in disbelief at the opacity
of some indefinite influence.

Caterpillar Train

The caterpillar train devours
the rail tracks in varying speeds.
Dwarf houses hidden in ignorance
like seventeenth century peasants
raise walls of burgeoning superstitions.
Towers of swinging electric wires
stand at ease in silent prayers.
The mystic fishplate becomes
the forgotten village dervish.
In the ocean of the night
memories birth and perish.
Somewhere far rows of colourful lights
remind me of happiness.
Somewhere far it is still day.

Room Cat

this cat that sits
in my room
is not a cat
it's a lifeless form
almost
but not quite
its skin a bag
its paws soft pads
sometimes I think
it's not the cat
but the room's
in the cat

Bubble Universe

the cinder burns
warmth wafts in the air
snuggles by your side

one warm chill
squirrels up your spine
reaches a dead end
in your head

lies illicit
until it escapes
into a bubble of thought

you smile at it
in a dark chamber
remember
amnesia
where you forget
to forget

Blindness

A pole tilts on stilled breeze,
a bare-branched tree laughs at the sky,
climbers climb down the fence in a rotten mass,
the metaled road mixes with the red path,
a caged fan flips the summer air under a bored light,
plants in pots hide sounds of sustenance,
behind the wind, wind-chimes rehearse being dead.
Blindness is the smell of coffee we never had.

Blind Man's Rainbow

"A great poet must have the ear of a wild Arab listening in the silent desert, the eye of a North American Indian tracing the footsteps of an enemy upon the leaves that strew the forest, the touch of a blind man feeling the face of a darling child."

Samuel Taylor Coleridge

There is something similar
in our poems, I tell you,
as if like siblings they have
a family resemblance.

I can't pin point this or that...
something hovers like a glow,
like a smell over our poems,
something that connects us two.

So when I feel far from you
and feelings overwhelm me,

I take out all our poems
and touch their shapes and contours,

just like a blind man feeling
the face of a darling child.

Forgetting the Rains

That day at Triangular Park
you read your poems to the streets
while it rained on the trees.
Under the carapace it always rains—
first a drizzle, then a shower.
Two drops of water dribble
and settle on a scooter seat but
their meniscuses don't meet.
The days become wet and sticky
like folded damp paper.
We soaked in those days
and the insides of our pockets
still retain the moisture.
The world changed unnoticed
somewhere in between.
The wetness on the road
was perhaps an accident.
Should I now call you my Kashmir
and make love political?
We have forgotten the rains.

Lake Bled

a lease of summer vacation
leads you to Europe again

under European skies clouds wriggle
into shapes from Constable's canvas

memory is a crippled cloud,
it cannot run away and escape

in Lake Bled nature's poetry swims
vermilion red, florescent green

on shimmering water shadows
shake in cursive calligraphy

towers quiver, mountains waver
into indistinguishable ciphers

the azure blends seamlessly
from the surface to the sky

memory skims and drowns
into life, into oblivion

Written at a Tea Stall on Sriniketan Road

post breakfast
there's something odd
amongst the sweat

maybe it's me
maybe not

water wears a bluish cloak
in the form of a jug

purple memories
of my brother's birthstone

he visited Tawang
long time back

back then memory used to be thin like rust

at Bumla Pass
the rugged beauty of the land
makes home in your heart

once more you undergo
a cleansing of the mind
build a monastery

someone knocks at the door
countries bicker
borders waver

a migrant soul
drowns in the lake
freezes in the snow

Rain Within

It is raining inside me
but you can't see.
Clouds of words enter me
but you can't see.

It always rains in Macondo,
do you know?
A hundred years of solitude inside me,
do you know?

You come back from a holiday in Venice,
too exhausted to enjoy the rains;
I stay quarantined in Oran,
too exhausted to enjoy the rains.

The precipitation inside me
dissolves my soul,
distills my tears,
dilates my heart,
dilutes my orgasm;
you know, you see,
but you are too exhausted
by all the rains without me.

Fugitive Words

I have jailed my heart,
no fugitive words
will escape from it
except in disguise
like these trespassers.

I have folded
your memory
like a starched bed sheet
of warping
and woofing threads.

I have risen
like a rock
to the stars,
burning, burning,
yet touching.

Now I can fly,
see, I can fly

with all the
paroled words
that scour the sky.

I have come
too close to beauty,
my eyes dazzle,
my vision fades
and I die young.

The Air That Ate Eternity

If
there were no air
between us
my fingers would have
poured into
the melting vacuum
and touched
the meniscus of your body
dissolving all resistance.
Every contour of your body
would have jigsawed
into the lines of my hands.
My fate
would have become a bird
and flown north.
The paradise in my mind
would have trembled in my eyes
and streamed out immortalized.
But,
there is air between us,
where whispers argue
that I lost you
even before
I found you.

Ajar

From a slight-parted window
light comes and settles in
my room at night. Lingers on
one wall for long. Staring
at my sleepless body. Soon
it will be dawn. Memory
too slightly parts my mind,
ruptures neurons, punctures brain;
every night, in stolen light,
bleeds unrequited like dew.
We don't forgive and forget,
we grow our love incomplete.

On that Moment of Horripilation when Our Cold Feet Touch

How beautiful is the thought of you!
Early morning a stray chill flies
like a harbinger of winter.
It buries itself in my head
and gets cozy and warm between the folds of my brain,
until,
under the cover of now and then
our cold feet touch,
memories horripilate
like apparitions from the dead.

I try to purge all thoughts of you,
the mind becomes empty as if nothing else exists.
Under the simmering surface of reflection
there is nothing absolutely selfless
that is not absolutely selfish.

Like a Tree

When I last saw you
you were in green,
remember?
And then there are eyes
and pass by days,
unseeing.
Remember the times
and many ways
of meeting?
We no longer meet
and still it rains
in the night.
What if the rains are
tears that lost
saltiness?
There's so much sadness,
sorrow and death
in this world.
But none finds a place
in my poems
about you.
And that is the drug
that makes me live
like a tree.

Transformation

Whenever I think of you,
there is a lump in my throat.
Whenever...
morning, afternoon, evening.
The problem is when people
ask me why I am silent
and I can't reply
because of the lump.
I have grown fond of it
because that is all
you have left behind,
that is all
that is left of you.
At night when there is no one
to question my silence
I make love to the lump
and it transforms
into a poem.

Olfaction

Tonight I decide to write
about the scent of the city
in your absence.
But I can't smell anything.
There are no rains,
there is no petrichor.
I never came close enough
to register your fragrance.
Days become months
and then there is an odour–
putrid, putrescent.
I know it is the stench of memory.
Tonight was long ago.
There is no city without you.
Imagine peeling an orange,
squeezing the peel,
and getting no odor.
It takes too much imagination.

Fronds

Nostalgia recalls
a bunch of summer days,
who come to look at me
when I don't look at them.
They peep into my room
through a curtained dawn
and when my eyes open
they scoot into the lanes.

I wake up missing you
my friend from other days.

Spring loiters in the mind
brewing secrets in its leaves,
unknown to the mewing cat
prowling the city streets.
A traffic light waits for change
in the seasons of the heart
while hope gathers fronds of
all afternooned summer days.

Shell

In a bright room
you find a shell,
house of a crustacean.
You put it to your ears
to listen to the sound
of the roaring seas.
I see it on your palm
and then the brightness
suddenly blinds me.
A woman vanishes,
a little girl vanishes,
leaving a house soundless.
On a rocking chair
I conjure nostalgias,
sleeping and dreaming.
Sounds of the shells
surround my dreams,
waking and breaking.
Waves of my sleep
curl into a silent
embryo of vacancy.

The Greatest Love Poem

Last night having failed to write
the greatest love poem of all times
I decide to write that failed poem
and question what is greatness.

Staring long at a grey patch of green,
it seems the greys are the greens
and ungreatness a greatness
and all deceiving undeceiving.

Isn't unbuilding walls great?
What else is I cannot say, perhaps,
all love should be common and
a poem is not meant to be great.

The City in the Night Time

The city in the night time
is very much the city
I left behind. What difference
does it make whether it is
Bolpur or Kolkata?
If I don't see it, it is
the same city where you are
awake late into the night
and reply to my queries.
That's our colourful secret,
secret as this poem is,
a poem no one can read.

The Last Obsession

A bunch of words then
was an obsession,
no longer so.
Now invisible
under water,
holding stones,
they lie low.
The only breath,
when a name's dropped
on the surface,
that too has left.
So silent it seeps
in the lungs of life
the twenty years
of living death.
So long I leant
on a pillar that
it thinks I have
no job to do.

Measuring Emptiness

Your busyness begets emptiness.
In the language of imagined
people I speak... Is this the sign
of madness or just being a poet?
In the language of imagined
people I measure emptiness.
A spoken word bounces from wall
to wall to wall to wall until it comes
back to me old and tired and
debilitating as if after a long
journey into dementia.
Some words don't return at all
and are reported missing
in the language I imagine.

The Water Diviner

Your words at the end of the week
beget a month of wordlessness

My words become a tourniquet
on my vacillating forehead

You are the gloaming of the day
slowly fading out on tiptoes

My solicitude becomes frail
as memories starve in the night

I, a water diviner, search
for a solvent to sustain life

A gossamer world spins a web
to entrap my unconsciousness

Building the Pacific Ocean

Tonight I can build the Pacific Ocean,
plunging into a buoyant darkness,
send sonars from my lips
to bounce at your depths.
I can dig deep and hold
water on pillars of patience.
On other days it may take years
but not tonight...
Tonight is the night when
grief consorts with delight,
an ailing body renews its cells
in an obstinate wait
at the placid surface
for a recalcitrant echo.

Spectrum

Autumn blesses you
with the last slice of sun.
Winter spreads
in bits and pieces.
Aftertaste of summer
lingers in memory.
Unseasonal rains
leave stranded wetness.
You debate on clothes
for a change.
Vanished mothballs
hang in their scent.
Wistful birds of mind
wish to fly.
All missing dreams are found
in jars of unslept sleep.
An orphan thought
longs for a different sky.

Windows

You find a dried-up yellow rose
inside the pages of a broken book.

The story of the broken rose
obscures the story of the yellow book.

One day my books with your words
will reach some unknown readers.

For them these will be the windows
full of sad exotic colours.

That's how we will be conjured up
when the age of magic wakes us.

Sleeping

When the last vestige of the night
spends its last breath
and I find that I have
slept all through it
and missed the Leonid shower,
I search the sky for Sagittarius.

On dark warm winter nights
when my grandmother's asthma
crawls into a street child's lungs
and wakes him up into paroxysms
of an impending death,
I recall how I have slept.

I recall how I have lived
when I was asleep
and how every awakening
has been a living death,
how every struggle to breathe in
is a constellation missing.

Saving the Bridge

The footbridge of unfooted dreams
lies limp in disuse. Today our
feet breathe. It's been a while since we
let our feet fly. Sometimes the sky
connects, sometimes the bridge divides.
Sometimes desires harden,
sometimes liquefy, sometimes
all the mist of remembrance
fades and you are desperate
to hang on to a hangover.
A housefly homes in on a cut fruit,
sits on it, you stare at it
long enough to forget the bridge
devoid of mist, devoid of feet,
devoid of a drunk homecoming.

The Lost Pigeons of Summer

When you think of the lost pigeons of summer
you also think of the lost time that will no
                          longer tick on wrists,
you also think of the monsoon that lost its way
                          in the mountains,
you also think of all the virtues that were taken
                          into quarantine,
you also think of all the words that became
                          sound and disappeared,
and you also think of all the lost poetry that will
                          remain lost poetry.
The lost pigeons of summer were lovers.
In the birdbath of loss their love was found.

Elephant

There is an elephant in my room.
I do not notice it.
It is dead.

A putrid smell from its body
spreads in the city.

I arrange my years around it.
I have one year too many.

That year I ask you to take home
for it was you who
killed the elephant
lurking in my room.

Now I do not notice it.
It is just a lump of dead memory.

Into the Darkness

Rains cease eventually
but not the darkness.
Clouds make the cat think
twice before it jumps
into a puddle.

Someone watches my
sadness grow dark.
Evening bursts from
the breasts into night.
A distant thunder
lowers its breath.
A stray dog barks
in utter contempt.

When it rains again
the first two drops will
touch my lips and I
will know the hard kiss
of someone's wetness.

Long Night

My nights are long.
Time stretches from second
to minute for hours.
Yet there is no time
to kiss or smoke.
This is how one feels
when one feels no more,
this is how the waves
crawl on the beaches,
this is how all sounds
collapse into spaces,
this is how the day
mourns unspent kisses,
this is how the rains
smoke out petrichor,
this is how it happened
when it did not happen.
This world an illusion,
where time stretches
into a slow death.

Small Hours

During small hours
a newsagent,
between small talk,
gives great news.
Small hours all dark
except a small bulb
and a gentle glow
in a small arc.
All news emanate,
some illuminate,
others are utter
worldly matters.
Small hours at Lethe,
small change for love,
for a little
forgetfulness.

The Tumour in My Head

The slack imagination
retards my affection.
A swift dragonfly flits
splitting the webbing
between what I dream
and what is real.
The curtain feels the wind,
shies into a flutter.
In utter embarrassment
the fan stutters in motion.
The light flickers, flickers
passing through the heat.
A rare wisp rises,
lives, dies, becomes
a speck of memory.
The long-winding day dawns,
the night no longer speaks.
The eyes become hives
of bees in business.
The unemployed poet,
consorting with faith,
dies a sudden death.
Once more his body becomes
one more tumor in my head.

About a Homicide

So I murdered my happiness.
The cloths of heaven cover my dreams.
A bullet lodges in my brain,
it does not pay any rent,
it sleeps and procreates
more bullets in my head.

A sad man stands accused
while the happy man escapes.
The sad man does not know his age.
He files for anticipatory bail,
the files fly slapping his face
and making his own jail.

At the trial the bullet speaks
of a fairy-tale homicide
of puncturing memories
and spilling laughter,
of split skulls of truth
and slit throats of contention,

of mashed up bones of love
and manslaughtered breaths.

The fingerprints of history
come like rows of waves,
they keep coming and coming
like a witness parade.

The jury deliberates,
pronounces the sad man guilty.
The shivering chill of winter
makes home his voice,
his hands turn senile
and can't hold much,
and his innards experience
volcanic throw ups.

Will the happy man never come back?
If the murderer was here
he would have witnessed
the making of a caricature.

Look, the sad man ruffles the water
and the ripples delete him little by little.

Lost Object

I have lived with your loss,
said the object I lost.
I have lived without your
familiar touch, care,
love and possessiveness.
I have lived abandoned,
desecrated, left alone
like a child without childhood.
I have lived on that side
of your forgetfulness
where the wounds of history
rupture into a sore.
I have lived with the others,
with the label 'owners lost',
in the nook of a cupboard
of the school you have left.
When you wake up from your sleep,
I sleep with your missing dream,
illicit in your mind
like a whore of the night.

Ruminations from a Sick Bed

Last Sunday
around 1:15 p.m.
I turned old.

A hundred butterflies
gathered for winter jamming
inside my left knee joint.

A couple of snakes
crossed over each other
inside my right foot.

The chair I sat on wobbled,
the spoon I ate with shivered
and the cat I chased stayed put.

The wind faintly carried
the odour of ointments
from my buckling body.

A sad black cardigan
hugged gently my white shirt
in a lonesome embrace.

My eyes strained to read
the fine print of that kid
who wrote his longings.

Winter wars have left me
with broken birthday candles
and an air of insanity.

Fermentation

Looking forward to old age
I migrate to the southern end of time,
let the birds of youth grow thin,
make hollow my bones of vintage desires,
cuddle your absence to sleep
entwined in the unbroken nest of dreams
and wait for your arrival
through the thinning marrow of time and space.

Extinction

My mind is gone where the birds have gone.
Some peace it has found where the birds have gone.

What happens to abducted love stories?
They are all unbound where the birds have gone.

All unkissed moments of our lives gather
As the sirens sound where the birds have gone.

In the nest of dreams twigs and memories
Each other confound where the birds have gone.

O Amit, your extinction is near.
We'll see you around where the birds have gone.

fugitive words | 98

The hush that descended after reading *Balconies of Time* never left. And into that silent space a few more fugitive words escaped. The stoic poet at night reveals layers of personal passions, social insights and aesthetic delight. The softness pierces the heart and wrenches the gut at the same time with a twist that is both beautiful and damning. Here is a poet of "negative capability" who finds his voice in the adverse time-space.

NOTES

The Waterfall
The poem was nominated for the Pushcart Prize in 2018 by *The Pangolin Review*.

A Warli Art
This poem was inspired by a painting done by M Padma Shri.

Convalescent
Totos are three-wheeled passenger vehicles.

The Three-Quarter Moon
Jahaji means one who has been on a ship.

This Bijoya
Kamala in Bengali means orange color. *Banalata Sen* is the protagonist of one of Jibananda Das's poems of the same name (1942). *Ashwin* is a month of the Bengali calendar when goddess Durga is worshipped. *Bijoya* is the last day of Durga Puja festival.

Grey Love
Hemanta hints at Autumn. *Basanta* insinuates Spring.

Rai
Rai is another name of Radha. *Basant Utsav* is the festival of Holi during spring season.

Brinda
Brinda is another name of Radha.

Binodini
Binodini is another name of Radha. *Saba* means a gentle breeze in Urdu. *Azaan* is the call for prayer for the Muslims. *Namaz* is the Muslim's prayer ritual. *Ghats* are the flight of steps leading down to a water body.

Lahore Bomb Blast Series
The Lahore bomb blast happened in March 2016.

The Hind Shawl Repairing House
Ripu is to repair a tear in clothes without a trace. *Refu* is a common mispronunciation of the word *Ripu* and does not belong to the standard Bengali lexicon. It is also a pun on the word refugee. *Chacha* means uncle in Hindi. *Kameez* is shirt.

Scattering
Mohona in Bengali means an estuary.

Rain Within
This poem, under the title "Rain Inside," was included in *Best Indian Poetry* 2018 anthology from *Hakara Journal*.

www.ingramcontent.com/pod-product-compliance
Lightning Source LLC
Chambersburg PA
CBHW031454040426
42444CB00007B/1092